Welcome to *Simple Pleasures of Convection Cooking*! On the following pages you'll discover 50 fresh-tasting, contemporary recipes designed to take full advantage of the ease, speed and versatility of your Jenn-Air dual-mode convection and bake/broil oven.

Choose from zesty appetizers, hearty main dishes, savory sides and luscious desserts. Each recipe bakes to perfection in the circulating air of the convection oven. Besides the recipes—listed with both convection and radiant baking directions—you'll find gorgeous photographs and helpful menu suggestions for family meals and special occasions, as well as lots of handy cooking tips.

This book was designed to help you take advantage of the many benefits of convection cooking, such as the timesaving convenience of three-rack baking. To learn more about the wonderful world of convection cooking, see the next page.

So head to the kitchen and try one of these mouthwatering recipes. You'll be delighted with the results. What's more, you'll be convinced, as we are, that cooking with a Jenn-Air convection oven is "The Sign of a Great Cook™"!

If you have any questions about the recipes in this book, please write: *Simple Pleasures of Convection Cooking*, 1912 Grand Avenue, Des Moines, IA 50309-3379.

ABOUT CONVECTION COOKING

Your versatile Jenn-Air convection oven is designed to handle just about any baking chore without a hitch. To help you get the most from your oven, here are some convection oven cooking facts and tips.

What Is Convection Cooking?

A convection oven is a radiant (conventional) oven with an important plus—a fan that keeps the hot air in the oven continuously moving. This prevents a layer of cooler air from surrounding the food and can speed up cooking by as much as 30 percent.

Besides cooking faster, convection ovens have several other advantages:

Strawberries

•Meats are juicier when roasted in the convection oven because the circulating air seals the surface and lets fewer juices escape.

•From-scratch breads are lighter, more evenly textured, more golden and crustier than those baked conventionally.

•Convection ovens can accommodate three-rack baking, which speeds up baking large quantities of foods and makes complete oven meals a breeze.

•By using a low temperature in a convection oven, you can oven-dry many foods.

Which Baking Pans Work Best?

For the most part, the same bakeware you use for radiant (conventional) baking will work well in your convection oven. Remember that dull, dark enameled or glass baking pans will make baked goods crusty and turn them a rich brown color. Shiny pans will give a lighter, more golden and tender crust. When choosing baking sheets, be sure to use the sheets without sides. These allow the air to circulate around the foods more evenly. Covered cookware can be used, however, you will not see a convection benefit because the air does not reach the food. Check your oven's use and care manual for the best sizes.

Helpful Hints

To use your convection oven most efficiently, keep these baking tips in mind:

•For the best browning results, your convection oven comes with two flat racks plus an offset rack that hangs below the rack guide. In the recipes in this book, the offset rack is designated by the word *offset* after the rack position number. The recipe directions will give you a specific position(s) for both flat and offset racks. (Starting at the bottom of the oven, the positions range from 1 to 4.) When using other recipes, refer to your oven's use and care manual for the best rack position(s).

•To avoid handling hot oven racks, arrange them before turning on the oven. If you'll be using more than one rack, space them as directed in your recipe or in your oven's use and care manual.

•Preheating is unnecessary for casseroles and roasts. Generally, only foods that bake a short time or those that require rising, browning or a crispy coating need to be baked in a preheated convection oven.

•Center foods in the oven, allowing about 1 to 1½ inches between the pans and the side walls of the oven for proper air circulation.

•When baking more than one pan, place the pans at opposite ends of the rack. Or stagger the pans on two racks so one pan does not shield the other.

•The best foods for baking on three racks include cookies, cupcakes, rolls, frozen convenience foods, pizzas, appetizers and snacks. You will need to allow additional baking time for items on the middle rack. Plan on 30 to 60 seconds additional baking time for thin foods, such as cookies, and 1 to 2 minutes more baking time for items such as biscuits, rolls or muffins.

•To keep the oven at a constant temperature and save energy, avoid opening the door frequently or keeping it open for a long time.

•Don't depend on baking time or surface brownness alone to judge doneness. Always test for doneness as directed in the recipe.

•When converting your radiant (conventional) oven recipes, follow these simple guidelines. 1.) Roast meats at the same temperature the conventional recipe suggests but reduce the roasting time. Time savings will depend on size of food being prepared—up to 30 percent for large turkeys. 2.) When baking, reduce oven temperature 25°F below the conventional temperature and reduce the time slightly. If you choose to use the same temperature for baking, you may experience some additional time savings.

•Refer to your oven's use and care manual for more information about recommended pan sizes, placement of baking pans and other features unique to your model.

Ginger Root

4

APPETIZERS

Turn a simple gathering into a memorable occasion with a variety of appetizers convection-baked to perfection. Take your pick of tiny cheese-filled tarts, crispy wontons, juicy chicken bites and more.

HERBED CHEESE TARTS

Create a colorful array by trimming each third of these luscious herb-flavored tarts with a different topper.

    Nonstick spray coating
⅓ cup fine dry bread crumbs (unseasoned)
    or fine zwieback crumbs
1 package (8 ounces) cream cheese,
    softened
¾ cup creamed cottage cheese
½ cup shredded Swiss cheese
1 tablespoon all-purpose flour
¼ teaspoon dried basil leaves
⅛ teaspoon garlic powder
2 eggs
    Dairy sour cream (optional)
    Sliced or slivered pitted ripe olives,
    slivered roasted red pepper or
    snipped fresh chives (optional)

Spray twenty-four 1¾-inch muffin cups with nonstick coating. Sprinkle bread crumbs onto bottom and sides of muffin cups to coat. Shake muffin pans to remove excess crumbs.

In small mixer bowl combine cream cheese, cottage cheese, Swiss cheese, flour, basil and garlic powder. Beat on medium speed of electric mixer just until fluffy. Add eggs. Beat on low speed just until combined. *Do not overbeat.*

Fill each muffin cup with 1 tablespoon cheese mixture. Bake in preheated 375°F **convection oven** on rack #2 or #3 offset for 9 to 10 minutes (or bake in preheated 375°F **radiant bake oven** 13 to 15 minutes) or until centers appear set. (Tarts will puff during baking, then deflate as they cool.) Cool in pans on wire racks 10 minutes. Remove from pans. Cool well.

To serve, spread with sour cream, if desired. Garnish with olives, red pepper or chives, if desired. Makes 24 appetizers (6 to 8 servings).

To make ahead: Bake and cool tarts as directed. Cover and chill up to 48 hours. Before serving, let chilled tarts stand at room temperature for 30 minutes. Serve as directed.

Nutrition facts per serving: 246 calories (69% from fat), 12 g protein, 7 g carbohydrates, 19 g fat, 0 g dietary fiber, 125 mg cholesterol, 310 mg sodium

THREE-TOMATO TART

Showcase this festive appetizer tart at your next party. It's great with a dry white wine or a flavored water.

1 recipe Single-Crust Pastry, page 28
3 tablespoons grated Parmesan cheese

Filling
2 egg whites, slightly beaten
1 cup ricotta cheese
1 clove garlic, minced
1 tablespoon snipped fresh thyme
    (or 1 teaspoon dried thyme leaves)
2 large tomatoes, sliced
5 yellow cherry tomatoes, sliced
2 red cherry tomatoes, sliced
1 tablespoon olive or vegetable oil
2 teaspoons snipped fresh thyme
    (or ½ teaspoon dried thyme leaves)

Prepare Single-Crust Pastry. On floured surface roll pastry to form 12-inch circle. Fit pastry into 10½-inch tart pan. Trim pastry even with rim. *Do not prick* pastry. Line with double thickness of foil. Bake in preheated 450°F **convection oven** on rack #2 or #3 offset for 5 minutes (or bake in preheated 450°F **radiant bake oven** 5 minutes). Remove foil. Bake 5 to 7 minutes more or until pastry is golden brown. Remove from oven. Reduce oven temperature to 375°F. Sprinkle tart shell with Parmesan cheese.

For filling: In small mixing bowl combine egg whites, ricotta cheese, garlic and 1 tablespoon thyme. Spread over Parmesan cheese in tart shell. Overlap large tomato slices in a circle around edge. Arrange yellow cherry tomato slices in circle within tomato ring. Fill center with red cherry tomato slices. Stir together olive oil and 2 teaspoons thyme. Brush mixture over tomatoes.

Bake in the 375°F **convection oven** 15 to 20 minutes (or bake in the 375°F **radiant bake oven** 20 to 25 minutes) or until heated through and nearly set. Cut into wedges. Serve warm or at room temperature. Makes 10 to 12 servings.

Nutrition facts per serving: 184 calories (53% from fat), 6 g protein, 15 g carbohydrates, 11 g fat, 1 g dietary fiber, 9 mg cholesterol, 133 mg sodium

Herbs

FOUR-CHEESE-AND-SPINACH TART

This elegant tart is so rich and satisfying, just a thin wedge is enough for a serving.

1   recipe Single-Crust Pastry, page 28
3   tablespoons fine dry bread crumbs (unseasoned)

Filling
1   egg, slightly beaten
½   cup ricotta cheese
½   cup shredded mozzarella cheese
½   cup shredded provolone cheese
3   tablespoons milk
2   tablespoons grated Parmesan or Romano cheese
⅛   teaspoon pepper
½   package (5 ounces) frozen chopped spinach, thawed and well drained
½   cup finely chopped salami

Pimiento (optional)
Sliced olives (optional)

Prepare Single-Crust Pastry. On floured surface roll pastry to form 11-inch circle. Fit pastry into 9-inch tart pan with removable bottom. Trim to ½ inch beyond edge. Fold extra pastry to inside and press against edge. *Do not prick* pastry. Line with double thickness of foil.

Bake in preheated 450°F **convection oven** on rack #2 or #3 offset for 5 minutes (or bake in preheated 450°F **radiant bake oven** 5 minutes). Remove foil. Bake 5 to 7 minutes more or until pastry is golden brown. Remove from oven. Reduce oven temperature to 375°F.

Sprinkle tart shell with bread crumbs.

For filling: In medium mixing bowl combine egg, ricotta cheese, mozzarella cheese, provolone cheese, milk, Parmesan cheese and pepper. Stir in spinach and salami. Carefully spoon over bread crumbs in tart shell.

Bake in the 375°F **convection oven** 20 to 25 minutes (or bake in the 375°F **radiant bake oven** 30 to 35 minutes) or until heated through and top is lightly browned. Garnish spinach tart with pimiento and sliced olives, if desired. Cut into wedges. Serve warm. Makes 10 to 12 servings.

Nutrition facts per serving: 217 calories (54% from fat), 9 g protein, 16 g carbohydrates, 13 g fat, 1 g dietary fiber, 39 mg cholesterol, 292 mg sodium

Eggs

CHICKEN-PESTO PINWHEELS

Pesto gives these delightful chicken and rye bread appetizers their robust flavor. Make a fresh spinach pesto, or buy refrigerated or bottled pesto.

4   skinless, boneless chicken breast halves (about 1 pound)
½   cup Spinach Pesto (below) or purchased pesto
Paprika
Rye or onion party bread slices
Dijon-style mustard

Rinse chicken and pat dry. Place each chicken piece between clear plastic wrap. Pound lightly with meat mallet to ¼-inch thickness. Remove plastic wrap.

Spread 2 tablespoons Spinach Pesto over each chicken piece. Roll up jellyroll style, starting from a short side. Place chicken rolls in ungreased 11x7-inch baking pan, seam side down. Brush with water. Sprinkle with paprika.

Bake in 350°F **convection oven** on rack #2 or #3 offset for 20 to 25 minutes (or bake in preheated 350°F **radiant bake oven** 25 to 30 minutes) or until chicken no longer is pink. Remove; cover and chill 4 to 24 hours.

To serve, cut chicken rolls into ¼-inch-thick slices. Diagonally cut each rye bread slice in half. Top bread triangles with Dijon-style mustard and chicken pinwheels. Makes about 48 appetizers (12 servings).

SPINACH PESTO: In blender or food-processor container place ½ cup toasted chopped *walnuts* or *pine nuts*. Cover and blend or process until very finely chopped. Transfer nuts to a bowl.

Place 2 cups loosely packed fresh *spinach leaves*, ⅓ cup *olive* or *vegetable oil* and 2 cloves *garlic*, minced, in blender or processor container. Cover and blend or process until smooth, stopping and scraping sides of container occasionally. Add 2 cups loosely packed fresh *basil leaves*. Cover and blend or process until smooth. Add to nuts. Stir in ½ cup grated *Parmesan* or *Romano cheese*.

To store leftover pesto, place in storage container. Cover tightly and chill up to 2 days or freeze up to 1 month. Makes 1 cup pesto.

Nutrition facts per serving: 167 calories (40% from fat), 13 g protein, 14 g carbohydrates, 8 g fat, 0 g dietary fiber, 26 mg cholesterol, 422 mg sodium

ORIENTAL PORK WONTONS

Skip deep-fat frying and rely on your convection oven to crisp these tasty bundles filled with pork and ginger.

Filling

8	ounces ground pork or raw chicken
½	cup shredded carrot
¼	cup finely chopped celery or water chestnuts
1	tablespoon soy sauce
1	tablespoon dry sherry
2	teaspoons cornstarch
2	teaspoons grated ginger root
½	package (8 ounces) wonton wrappers
2	tablespoons margarine or butter, melted Plum or sweet-and-sour sauce (optional)

For filling: In medium skillet cook and stir ground pork until no longer pink. Drain well. Stir in carrot, celery, soy sauce, sherry, cornstarch and ginger root.

Spoon 1 heaping teaspoon filling in center of a wonton wrapper. Lightly brush edges with water.

Carefully bring 2 opposite points of square wrapper up over filling and pinch together in center. Carefully bring remaining 2 opposite points to center and pinch together. Pinch together edges to seal. Place wontons on greased large baking sheet. Repeat with remaining filling and wonton wrappers.

Brush wontons with melted margarine. Bake in preheated 375°F **convection oven** on rack #2 or #3 offset for 5 to 7 minutes (or bake in preheated 375°F **radiant bake oven** 8 to 10 minutes) or until wontons are light brown and crisp. Serve wontons with plum sauce, if desired. Makes about 24 appetizers (8 servings).

To make ahead: Bake appetizers as directed; cool completely. Cover and chill overnight or freeze up to 1 month. To serve, place chilled or frozen wontons on greased large baking sheet. Bake in preheated 375°F **convection oven** on rack #2 or #3 offset for 5 to 7 minutes (or bake in preheated 375°F **radiant bake oven** 8 to 10 minutes) or until wontons are light brown and crisp.

Nutrition facts per serving: 169 calories (35% from fat), 8 g protein, 18 g carbohydrates, 6 g fat, 0 g dietary fiber, 23 mg cholesterol, 337 mg sodium

CRISPY CHICKEN BITES

Accent these juicy, tender nuggets with one or both of the flavor-packed dipping sauces.

1	pound skinless, boneless chicken thighs or breast halves
¼	cup all-purpose flour
1	teaspoon dried parsley flakes
½	teaspoon poultry seasoning
⅛	teaspoon salt
	Dash pepper
1	egg, beaten
2	tablespoons milk
1¼	cups whole-wheat or buttery round cracker crumbs
1	recipe Spiced Cherry Dipping Sauce or Cajun Dipping Sauce (below)

Rinse chicken and pat dry. Cut chicken into 1-inch pieces. In plastic bag combine flour, parsley flakes, poultry seasoning, salt and pepper. Add chicken pieces, a few at a time, to flour mixture. Close bag and shake to coat chicken pieces well. Remove chicken pieces and set aside. Repeat with remaining chicken.

In small mixing bowl combine beaten egg and milk. In another small bowl place cracker crumbs. Dip chicken, about ¼ of the pieces at a time, into egg mixture. Roll chicken pieces in cracker crumbs to coat.

Place coated chicken pieces in a single layer on ungreased large baking sheet. Bake in preheated 400°F **convection oven** on rack #2 or #3 offset for 6 to 8 minutes (or bake in preheated 400°F **radiant bake oven** 10 to 12 minutes) or until chicken no longer is pink. Serve appetizers with dipping sauce. Makes 8 servings.

SPICED CHERRY DIPPING SAUCE: In small saucepan combine 1 jar (12 ounces) *cherry jelly*, 2 tablespoons *lemon juice*, ⅛ teaspoon *ground mace* and dash *ground cloves*. Cook and stir over medium heat until heated through. Makes about 1 cup.

Nutrition facts per serving (chicken with cherry sauce): 315 calories (26% from fat), 14 g protein, 45 g carbohydrates, 9 g fat, 1 g dietary fiber, 71 mg cholesterol, 250 mg sodium

CAJUN DIPPING SAUCE: In blender container place 1 can (14½ ounces) *Cajun-style stewed tomatoes*. Cover and blend until nearly smooth. In medium saucepan combine blended tomatoes and 2 teaspoons *cornstarch*. Cook and stir until thickened and bubbly. Cook and stir 2 minutes more. Stir in ¼ teaspoon bottled *hot pepper sauce*. Makes 1½ cups.

Nutrition facts per serving (chicken with Cajun sauce): 184 calories (36% from fat), 14 g protein, 16 g carbohydrates, 7 g fat, 2 g dietary fiber, 67 mg cholesterol, 341 mg sodium

MENU

Appetizer Party
Serves 8 to 10

Chicken-Pesto Pinwheels
(opposite)

Four-Cheese-and-Spinach Tart
(opposite)

Oriental Pork Wontons
(at left)

Purchased dip(s) with fresh vegetable dippers

Fresh melon balls, strawberries and pineapple chunks

Assorted beverages

Delectable finger foods are just right for casual entertaining. To keep last-minute work to a minimum, the day before the party make the pinwheels and wontons and cut up the vegetables and fruits. Offer a selection of wines, liquors and nonalcoholic beverages, such as fruit juices or bottled mineral water.

MAIN DISHES

Whether you're looking for family fare or fine dining, you can create it in your convection oven—from the simple beauty of Potato-Topped Chicken to the elegance of Pork Roast with Pesto Stuffing.

PORK ROAST WITH PESTO STUFFING

The rich stuffing made with pesto and dried tomatoes complements the tender meat perfectly in this company-special roast. If your gathering is crowd-size, double the recipe to make two roasts.

Stuffing
½   cup plain croutons, slightly crushed
½   cup purchased pesto or Spinach Pesto, page 6
¼   cup chopped dried tomatoes* or pimiento

1   3- to 4-pound pork loin center rib roast, backbone loosened (6 ribs total)
    Fennel bulb tops (optional)

For stuffing: In small mixing bowl combine croutons, pesto and dried tomatoes. Set aside.

Place pork roast on cutting surface, rib side down. On meaty side, cut a 3½-inch-long and 1-inch-deep pocket lengthwise above each rib, making 6 pockets total. Spoon pesto stuffing into pockets.

Place stuffed roast in shallow roasting pan, rib side down. Sprinkle with a little salt and pepper. Insert meat thermometer into thickest portion of pork roast.

Bake in 325°F **convection oven** on rack #2 or #3 offset for 1¼ to 2 hours (or bake in 325°F **radiant bake oven** 1½ to 2¼ hours) or until thermometer registers 160°F. If necessary, cover with foil after 1 hour to prevent overbrowning. Let stand, covered, 15 minutes before carving.

Garnish serving platter with fennel bulb tops, if desired. To serve, slice pork roast between ribs. Makes 6 servings.

*If using oil-packed dried tomatoes, drain before chopping. If using dry-packed dried tomatoes, cover chopped tomatoes with boiling water. Let stand 10 minutes. Drain well.

Nutrition facts per serving: 391 calories (58% from fat), 34 g protein, 6 g carbohydrates, 25 g fat, 0 g dietary fiber, 91 mg cholesterol, 219 mg sodium

CORN-STUFFED PORK CHOPS

The currant jelly glazes these plump vegetable-stuffed chops to a beautiful golden brown. If you like, use strawberry or raspberry jelly instead.

4   pork loin rib chops, cut 1 inch thick (1½ to 1¾ pounds)

Stuffing
⅓   cup chopped onion
3   tablespoons chopped green pepper
3   tablespoons water
1   slice whole-wheat or rye bread, toasted and cubed
⅓   cup frozen whole-kernel corn
1   tablespoon chopped pimiento
¼   teaspoon ground cumin
⅛   teaspoon salt
⅛   teaspoon pepper

1   tablespoon currant jelly, melted
    Fresh parsley sprigs (optional)
    Marigolds* (optional)

Make a pocket in each pork chop by cutting horizontally into the pork chop from fat side almost to bone.

For stuffing: In saucepan stir together onion, green pepper and water. Heat to boiling; reduce heat. Cover and simmer 3 to 4 minutes or until vegetables are tender. *Do not drain.*

In small mixing bowl stir together bread cubes, corn, pimiento, cumin, salt and pepper. Add cooked vegetable mixture; toss lightly.

Spoon about ¼ cup stuffing into each pocket. If necessary, securely fasten opening with wooden toothpicks. Place on rack in shallow roasting pan. Sprinkle with salt and pepper.

Bake in preheated 350°F **convection oven** on rack #2 or #3 offset for 20 to 25 minutes (or bake in preheated 350°F **radiant bake oven** 35 to 40 minutes) or until pork no longer is pink. Brush with jelly the last 10 minutes of baking.

Garnish with parsley sprigs and marigolds, if desired. Makes 4 servings.

*Be sure to use *Targetes* species of marigolds that are free of chemicals.

Nutrition facts per serving: 208 calories (40% from fat), 20 g protein, 12 g carbohydrates, 9 g fat, 1 g dietary fiber, 50 mg cholesterol, 145 mg sodium

Corn-Stuffed Pork Chops

ORANGE-GINGER PORK CHOPS

Marinating the chops adds a delightful hint of orange, soy and ginger.

Marinade
½ cup orange juice
⅓ cup soy sauce
2 tablespoons orange marmalade
½ teaspoon ground ginger
½ teaspoon onion powder
¼ teaspoon garlic powder

4 boneless pork sirloin chops,
    1 inch thick
    Green onion fans (optional)
    Plum sauce, heated (optional)

For marinade: Stir together orange juice, soy sauce, orange marmalade, ginger, onion powder and garlic powder.

Place chops in large plastic bag or in baking dish. Add marinade. Secure bag or cover dish. Refrigerate at least 6 hours or overnight, turning occasionally.

Remove chops and reserve marinade. In small saucepan heat marinade to boiling. Set aside.

Place chops on rack in shallow roasting pan. Bake in preheated 350°F **convection oven** on rack #2 or #3 offset for 25 to 30 minutes (or bake in preheated 350°F **radiant bake oven** 35 to 40 minutes) or until pork no longer is pink, turning and brushing once with marinade.

Arrange chops on platter. Garnish with green onion fans, if desired. Pass warm plum sauce with chops, if desired. Makes 4 servings.

*Nutrition facts per serving:
313 calories (29% from fat), 42 g
protein, 12 g carbohydrates,
10 g fat, 0 g dietary fiber,
130 mg cholesterol,
1450 mg sodium*

Oranges

GLAZED HAM WITH ORANGE-HONEY SAUCE

The pleasant blend of marmalade, honey and mustard in the golden sauce gives the ham just the right touch of sweetness.

1 2- to 2½-pound fully cooked boneless
    half ham

Sauce
¼ cup orange juice
2 tablespoons honey
1 tablespoon prepared mustard
¼ cup chicken broth
2 teaspoons cornstarch
⅓ cup orange marmalade

    Curly endive (optional)
    Orange slices, halved (optional)

Make diagonal cuts about ¼ inch deep and 1 inch apart on top of ham. Place ham on rack in shallow roasting pan. Insert meat thermometer into thickest portion of meat.

Bake in 325°F **convection oven** on rack #2 offset for 1 hour (or bake in 325°F **radiant bake oven** 1¼ hours).

Meanwhile, for sauce: In small saucepan combine 2 tablespoons orange juice, the honey and mustard. Heat to boiling; remove from heat.

Brush ham with half of the honey mixture. Bake 15 to 25 minutes more or until thermometer registers 140°F.

Combine remaining orange juice, the chicken broth and cornstarch. Stir into remaining honey mixture. Cook and stir until thickened and bubbly. Cook and stir 2 minutes more. Stir in orange marmalade; heat through.

Slice ham and arrange on serving platter. Garnish with curly endive and orange slices, if desired. Pass orange-honey sauce with ham. Makes 8 to 10 servings.

Nutrition facts per serving: 234 calories (25% from fat), 29 g protein, 15 g carbohydrates, 6 g fat, 0 g dietary fiber, 62 mg cholesterol, 1566 mg sodium

CHOOSE-A-FILLING CALZONES

Tuck a scrumptious sausage, ham or chicken filling inside these easy sandwich pockets.

1 package (10 ounces) refrigerated pizza dough
1 recipe Sausage-Mushroom Filling, Ham-Spinach Filling or Chicken-Olive Filling (below)
1 egg, beaten with 1 teaspoon water
Grated Parmesan cheese (optional)

Unroll pizza dough. Stretch dough into 15x10-inch rectangle. Cut into six 5-inch squares.

Divide desired filling among squares. Brush edges with water. Lift one corner and stretch dough over to opposite corner. Press edges of dough well with tines of fork to seal.

Arrange on greased large baking sheet. Prick tops with fork. Brush with egg mixture. Sprinkle with Parmesan cheese, if desired.

Bake in preheated 425°F **convection oven** on rack #2 or #3 offset for 6 to 8 minutes (or bake in preheated 425°F **radiant bake oven** 8 to 10 minutes) or until golden brown.

Let calzones stand 5 minutes before serving. Makes 6 servings.

SAUSAGE-MUSHROOM FILLING: In large skillet cook 12 ounces *bulk pork or Italian sausage* until no longer pink. Drain. Stir in ½ cup *pizza sauce.* Stir in 1 cup shredded *mozzarella cheese* and 1 can (2 ounces) *mushroom stems and pieces,* drained.

Nutrition facts per serving (calzone with sausage filling): 321 calories (45% from fat), 18 g protein, 24 g carbohydrates, 16 g fat, 0 g dietary fiber, 75 mg cholesterol, 809 mg sodium

HAM-SPINACH FILLING: Cook 1 package (10 ounces) frozen *chopped spinach* according to package directions. Drain well. In medium mixing bowl combine spinach, 1 cup finely chopped *fully cooked ham,* 1 cup shredded *Swiss cheese* and 2 tablespoons thinly sliced *green onion.*

Nutrition facts per serving (calzone with ham filling): 250 calories (31% from fat), 18 g protein, 25 g carbohydrates, 9 g fat, 1 g dietary fiber, 65 mg cholesterol, 634 mg sodium

CHICKEN-OLIVE FILLING: In medium bowl combine 1½ cups diced *cooked chicken,* ½ cup shredded *Monterey Jack cheese,* ¼ cup finely chopped *celery,* ¼ cup chopped *pitted ripe olives,* ½ teaspoon dried *basil leaves,* ¼ teaspoon *garlic salt* and ⅛ teaspoon *pepper.* Stir in ⅓ cup *soft-style cream cheese with chives and onion.*

Nutrition facts per serving (calzone with chicken filling): 279 calories (37% from fat), 19 g protein, 24 g carbohydrates, 11 g fat, 0 g dietary fiber, 74 mg cholesterol, 504 mg sodium

SAUSAGE AND MUSHROOM PASTA PIE

If you enjoy fiery foods, make this savory main-dish pie with hot Italian sausage.

Crust
4 ounces packaged spaghetti
1 egg, beaten
⅓ cup grated Parmesan or Romano cheese
1 tablespoon margarine or butter

Filling
1 egg, beaten
1 cup creamed cottage cheese
1 tablespoon snipped fresh parsley
1 can (4 ounces) sliced mushrooms, drained
12 ounces bulk Italian or pork sausage
½ cup chopped onion
¼ cup chopped green pepper
1 cup meatless spaghetti sauce
¼ teaspoon garlic powder
1 tablespoon grated Parmesan or Romano cheese

½ cup shredded mozzarella cheese

For crust: Cook spaghetti according to package directions. Drain. In medium mixing bowl combine 1 egg, ⅓ cup Parmesan cheese and margarine. Stir in hot spaghetti. Press mixture evenly into bottom and up sides of greased 9-inch pie plate. Set aside.

For filling: In small mixing bowl stir together 1 egg, cottage cheese and parsley. Spread mixture evenly over crust. Sprinkle with mushrooms.

In large skillet cook sausage, onion and green pepper until sausage no longer is pink. Drain well. Stir in spaghetti sauce and garlic powder. Heat through. Spoon meat mixture over cottage cheese mixture. Sprinkle with 1 tablespoon Parmesan cheese.

Bake in 350°F **convection oven** on rack #2 or #3 offset for 20 to 25 minutes (or bake in preheated 350°F **radiant bake oven** 23 to 25 minutes) or until filling is heated through.

Sprinkle with mozzarella cheese. Let stand 5 minutes. Cut into wedges. Makes 5 servings.

Nutrition facts per serving: 442 calories (50% from fat), 28 g protein, 28 g carbohydrates, 25 g fat, 2 g dietary fiber, 139 mg cholesterol, 1199 mg sodium

CRISPY BAKED HALIBUT

Swordfish or shark steaks also are delicious with this golden herb and cheese coating.

1¼   pounds fresh or frozen halibut steaks, cut 1 inch thick, or 4 skinless, boneless chicken breast halves (about 1 pound)
2   teaspoons vegetable oil

Coating
¾   cup soft sourdough or other bread crumbs
2   tablespoons grated Parmesan cheese
1   tablespoon snipped fresh marjoram (or 1 teaspoon dried marjoram leaves)
½   teaspoon paprika
    Dash pepper

    Fresh marjoram sprigs (optional)
    Lime wedges (optional)

Thaw fish, if frozen. Cut fish into 4 serving-size portions. Pat dry with paper towels. Brush with vegetable oil.

For coating: In shallow dish stir together bread crumbs, Parmesan cheese, snipped marjoram, paprika and pepper.

Dip fish or chicken into coating to cover both sides evenly. Arrange pieces in ungreased 2-quart rectangular baking dish. Sprinkle any leftover coating on top of fish or chicken.

For fish: Bake in preheated 450°F **convection oven** on rack #2 or #3 offset for 9 to 11 minutes (or bake in preheated 450°F **radiant bake oven** 10 to 12 minutes) or until fish just flakes easily with a fork.

For chicken: Bake in preheated 450°F **convection oven** on rack #2 or #3 offset for 12 to 15 minutes (or bake in preheated 450°F **radiant bake oven** 14 to 16 minutes) or until chicken no longer is pink.

Garnish with marjoram sprigs and serve with lime wedges, if desired. Makes 4 servings.

Nutrition facts per serving: 157 calories (33% from fat), 21 g protein, 5 g carbohydrates, 6 g fat, 0 g dietary fiber, 3 mg cholesterol, 150 mg sodium

Lemons and Limes

RICE-AND-RAISIN-STUFFED SALMON

Dried porcini mushrooms—sometimes called cèpes—have a woodsy, nutlike flavor. Look for them in the produce section of your supermarket or at a specialty-foods store.

Stuffing
8   dried porcini or oyster mushrooms
½   cup chopped onion
1   clove garlic, minced
2   tablespoons margarine or butter
1¼   cups regular brown rice
⅓   cup wild rice, rinsed and drained
3½   cups chicken broth
2   tablespoons snipped fresh thyme (or 1 teaspoon dried thyme leaves)
¼   teaspoon pepper
½   cup light raisins

1   3½- to 4-pound whole dressed salmon (with tail)
1   tablespoon olive or vegetable oil
    Fresh dill (optional)
    Lemon peel strips (optional)

For stuffing: In small bowl cover dried mushrooms with warm water. Let stand 30 minutes. Drain well and chop mushrooms.

Meanwhile, in large saucepan sauté onion and garlic in margarine until onion is tender. Add brown rice and wild rice. Cook and stir 2 minutes more.

Stir chicken broth, thyme and pepper into rice mixture. Heat to boiling; reduce heat. Cover and simmer 40 to 45 minutes or until rice is tender. Stir in raisins and dried mushrooms.

Fill fish cavity with 1 cup stuffing. Tie or skewer fish closed. Place stuffed fish on greased rack in large shallow baking pan. (If necessary, trim tail to fit.) Brush outside of fish with olive oil. Spoon remaining stuffing into ungreased 1½-quart casserole; cover casserole.

Bake fish on rack #2 offset and stuffing in casserole on rack #3 in 350°F **convection oven** 45 to 50 minutes (or bake fish and stuffing in casserole in preheated 350°F **radiant bake oven** 50 to 60 minutes) or until fish just flakes easily with a fork.

Garnish fish with dill and lemon peel strips, if desired. Makes 8 servings.

Nutrition facts per serving: 444 calories (35% from fat), 32 g protein, 40 g carbohydrates, 17 g fat, 3 g dietary fiber, 86 mg cholesterol, 515 mg sodium

TOASTED ALMOND AND GINGER FILLETS

For a great-tasting, easy-to-fix supper, team these nutty fish fillets with buttered French-style green beans and quick-cooking brown rice.

1   pound fresh or frozen orange roughy or lake trout fillets, ½ to ¾ inch thick
    Nonstick spray coating
1   tablespoon milk

Topping
¼   cup seasoned fine dry bread crumbs
1   to 1½ teaspoons grated ginger root
¼   cup sliced almonds or chopped peanuts
2   tablespoons margarine or butter, melted

    Lemon slices, halved (optional)

Thaw fish, if frozen. Cut fish into 4 serving-size portions. Spray 2-quart rectangular baking dish with nonstick coating.

Arrange fish in baking dish, turning under any thin edges so fish is a uniform thickness. Brush with milk.

For topping: In small dish combine bread crumbs and ginger root. Sprinkle crumb mixture and almonds over fish, covering entire surface of fish evenly. Drizzle with melted margarine.

Bake in preheated 450°F **convection oven** on rack #2 or #3 offset for 6 to 9 minutes (or bake in preheated 450°F **radiant bake oven** 8 to 12 minutes) or until topping is golden brown and fish just flakes easily with a fork.

Serve baked fish fillets with lemon slices, if desired. Makes 4 servings.

Nutrition facts per serving: 169 calories (52% from fat), 14 g protein, 6 g carbohydrates, 10 g fat, 1 g dietary fiber, 17 mg cholesterol, 268 mg sodium

BAKED SOLE AND CORN SALSA

Spicy salsa is a flavorful contrast to delicate sole in this easy entrée. Use hot, medium or mild salsa to suit your taste.

1   pound fresh or frozen sole, flounder or haddock fillets, ½ to ¾ inch thick
    Nonstick spray coating

Topping
1½ cups salsa
½   cup frozen whole-kernel corn

    Fresh cilantro or parsley sprigs (optional)

Thaw fish, if frozen. Cut fish into 4 serving-size portions. Spray 2-quart rectangular baking dish with nonstick coating. Arrange fish in baking dish, turning under any thin edges so fish is a uniform thickness.

For topping: In small bowl combine salsa and frozen corn. Spoon topping over fish, covering entire surface of fish evenly.

Bake in preheated 375°F **convection oven** on rack #2 or #3 offset for 14 to 16 minutes (or bake in preheated 375°F **radiant bake oven** 20 to 25 minutes) or until fish just flakes easily with a fork.

Using slotted spatula, transfer fish and salsa topping to dinner plates. Garnish with cilantro, if desired. Makes 4 servings.

Nutrition facts per serving: 123 calories (9% from fat), 17 g protein, 11 g carbohydrates, 1 g fat, 1 g dietary fiber, 43 mg cholesterol, 645 mg sodium

BAKED DEVILED SALMON FILLETS

Salmon fillets are sure to be a favorite when topped with this tangy sauce made with tarragon and cream cheese.

1½   pounds fresh or frozen salmon or orange roughy fillets, ½ to ¾ inch thick, or 1¾ pounds fresh or frozen salmon, swordfish or halibut steaks, 1 inch thick

Topping
- ½   package (4 ounces) cream cheese, softened
- 1   tablespoon mayonnaise or salad dressing
- 1   tablespoon milk
- 1½   teaspoons dry onion soup mix
- 1½   teaspoons lemon juice
- ½   teaspoon dried tarragon leaves
- ½   teaspoon Dijon-style mustard

Crumbs
- ¾   cup soft whole-wheat bread crumbs
- ½   cup snipped fresh parsley
- ¼   cup grated Parmesan cheese
- ½   teaspoon paprika

Lemon twists (optional)
Fresh tarragon sprigs (optional)

Thaw fish, if frozen. Cut fish into 6 serving-size portions. Arrange fish in single layer in greased shallow baking pan, turning under any thin edges of fillets so fish is a uniform thickness.

For topping: In small bowl combine cream cheese, mayonnaise, milk, onion soup mix, lemon juice, dried tarragon and Dijon mustard. (Mixture may appear slightly lumpy.) Spread topping evenly over surface of fish.

Bake in preheated 450°F **convection oven** on rack #2 or #3 offset for 9 to 10 minutes for fillets, 13 to 15 minutes for steaks (or bake in preheated 450°F **radiant bake oven** 10 to 12 minutes for fillets, 14 to 16 minutes for steaks) or until fish *almost* flakes with a fork.

Meanwhile, for crumbs: In small bowl combine bread crumbs, parsley, Parmesan cheese and paprika. Sprinkle crumbs over fish.

Bake 2 to 3 minutes more or until crumbs are golden and fish just flakes easily with a fork.

Garnish with lemon twists and tarragon sprigs, if desired. Makes 6 servings.

Nutrition facts per serving: 306 calories (58% from fat), 27 g protein, 5 g carbohydrates, 19 g fat, 1 g dietary fiber, 100 mg cholesterol, 303 mg sodium

Baked Deviled Salmon Fillets

WINE-AND-HERB-MARINATED PRIME RIB

Thanks to minimal last-minute preparation, this hearty beef roast allows you plenty of time to prepare the rest of the meal.

Marinade
¾ cup dry red wine
½ cup chopped onion
¼ cup lemon juice
¼ cup water
1 tablespoon Worcestershire sauce
½ teaspoon dried rosemary leaves
½ teaspoon dried marjoram leaves
¼ teaspoon garlic salt

1 4- to 6-pound beef rib roast
    Fresh rosemary sprigs (optional)

For marinade: In medium mixing bowl stir together red wine, onion, lemon juice, water, Worcestershire sauce, dried rosemary, marjoram and garlic salt.

Place meat in large plastic bag or in baking dish. Add marinade. Secure bag or cover dish. Refrigerate at least 6 hours or overnight, turning occasionally.

Remove meat and discard marinade. Place meat in shallow roasting pan, fat side up. Insert meat thermometer into center of meat.

Bake in 325°F **convection oven** on rack #2 offset for 1¾ to 2¼ hours for medium-rare (145°F) or 2 to 2¾ hours for medium (160°F). [Or bake in 325°F **radiant bake oven** 2 to 3 hours for medium-rare (145°F) or 2¼ to 3¾ hours for medium (160°F).]

If necessary, cover meat with foil the last 30 minutes to prevent overbrowning.

Let meat stand, covered, 15 minutes before carving. Garnish with fresh rosemary sprigs, if desired. Makes 12 to 16 servings.

Nutrition facts per serving: 261 calories (51% from fat), 28 g protein, 3 g carbohydrates, 14 g fat, 0 g dietary fiber, 81 mg cholesterol, 645 mg sodium

BEEF WITH DIJON MUSTARD GRAVY

This flavorful gravy cuts the fat but none of the flavor by starting with beef broth instead of meat drippings. Enjoy the gravy also with broiled or grilled steaks, hamburgers or pork chops.

1 2- to 3-pound beef eye round roast

Gravy
1 cup beef broth
1 tablespoon cornstarch
1 tablespoon Dijon-style mustard
1 teaspoon honey
1 teaspoon Worcestershire sauce

    Snipped fresh chives (optional)

Place meat on rack in shallow roasting pan. Insert meat thermometer into center of meat.

Bake in 325°F **convection oven** on rack #2 offset for 1 to 1½ hours for medium-rare (145°F) or 1½ to 2 hours for medium (160°F). [Or bake in 325°F **radiant bake oven** 1¼ to 1¾ hours for medium-rare (145°F) or 1¾ to 2¼ hours for medium (160°F).]

For gravy: In small saucepan combine beef broth, cornstarch, Dijon mustard, honey and Worcestershire sauce. Cook and stir over medium heat until sauce is thickened and bubbly. Cook and stir 2 minutes more.

Slice meat and arrange on serving platter. Garnish mustard gravy with chives, if desired. Pass gravy with meat. Makes 8 to 10 servings.

Nutrition facts per serving: 161 calories (30% from fat), 25 g protein, 3 g carbohydrates, 5 g fat, 0 g dietary fiber, 59 mg cholesterol, 221 mg sodium

Roast Chicken Tarragon

Also use this zesty tarragon, mustard and yogurt brush-on to dress up baked chicken pieces or Cornish hens.

1   2½- to 3-pound whole broiler-fryer
     chicken

Topping
¼   cup plain yogurt
1   tablespoon prepared mustard
1   teaspoon dried tarragon, thyme or
     basil leaves

     Lemon leaves (optional)
     Lemon wedges (optional)

Rinse chicken and pat dry. Skewer neck skin to back. Tie drumsticks to tail. Twist wing tips under back. Place chicken on rack in shallow roasting pan, breast side up.

For topping: In small mixing bowl stir together yogurt, mustard and tarragon. Brush topping evenly onto chicken. Insert meat thermometer into center of a thigh.

Bake in 375°F **convection oven** on rack #2 offset for 60 to 70 minutes (or bake in 375°F **radiant bake oven** 1¼ to 1½ hours) or until thermometer registers 180° to 185°F and drumsticks move easily.

If necessary, cover chicken with foil the last 10 to 20 minutes to prevent overbrowning.

Let stand, covered, 10 minutes before carving. Garnish with lemon leaves and lemon wedges, if desired. Makes 4 servings.

Nutrition facts per serving: 352 calories (52% from fat), 40 g protein, 1 g carbohydrates, 20 g fat, 0 g dietary fiber, 126 mg cholesterol, 176 mg sodium

Southwestern-Style Roast Chicken

A black-bean salsa accents this beautifully browned, herb-rubbed chicken (pictured on the cover). Freshly baked corn bread is a tasty Southwestern accompaniment.

1   4- to 5-pound whole roasting chicken
1   tablespoon olive or vegetable oil
1   teaspoon dried oregano leaves
½   teaspoon ground cumin
1   lime, cut into 6 wedges
2   fresh cilantro sprigs

Salsa
1   can (15 ounces) black beans, rinsed
     and drained
1   small tomato, chopped
1   small cucumber, seeded and chopped
¼   cup chopped green onions
2   tablespoons snipped fresh cilantro
     or parsley
1   teaspoon grated lime peel
2   tablespoons lime juice
1   tablespoon olive or vegetable oil
1   clove garlic, minced
¼   teaspoon salt

     Fresh oregano sprigs (optional)
     Tomato wedges (optional)
     Lime twists (optional)

Rinse chicken and pat dry. Brush with 1 tablespoon olive oil. Combine dried oregano and cumin. Sprinkle over outside of chicken, then rub into skin. Place lime wedges and cilantro sprigs in body cavity. Skewer neck skin to back. Tuck drumsticks under band of skin across tail or tie drumsticks to tail. Twist wing tips under back.

Place chicken on rack in shallow roasting pan, breast side up. Insert meat thermometer into center of a thigh.

Bake in 375°F **convection oven** on rack #2 offset for 1¼ to 1¾ hours (or bake in 375°F **radiant bake oven** 1½ to 2 hours) or until thermometer registers 180° to 185°F and drumsticks move easily. When chicken is two-thirds done, cut skin or string between drumsticks.

Meanwhile, for salsa: In medium bowl combine black beans, chopped tomato, cucumber, green onions, snipped cilantro, lime peel, lime juice, 1 tablespoon oil, garlic and salt. Mix well. Cover and chill until serving time.

Remove chicken from oven. Let stand, covered, 10 minutes before carving. Serve with salsa. Garnish with oregano sprigs, tomato wedges and lime twists, if desired. Makes 6 to 8 servings.

Nutrition facts per serving: 474 calories (49% from fat), 46 g protein, 14 g carbohydrates, 26 g fat, 3 g dietary fiber, 133 mg cholesterol, 305 mg sodium

CHEESE-STUFFED CHICKEN ROLLS

Look for the dried tomatoes in your supermarket's produce section. The tang they add to foods is irresistible.

2 tablespoons finely chopped dried tomatoes (not oil pack)
4 skinless, boneless chicken breast halves (about 1 pound)
2 tablespoons all-purpose flour
¼ teaspoon salt
⅛ teaspoon pepper
⅓ cup fine dry bread crumbs (unseasoned)
2 tablespoons grated Parmesan cheese
½ teaspoon paprika
1 egg, slightly beaten
4 ounces sharp Cheddar cheese
½ to 1 teaspoon dried fines herbes or sage leaves
1 tablespoon margarine or butter, melted

In small bowl cover dried tomatoes with boiling water. Let stand 10 minutes. Drain and pat dry. Set aside.

Rinse chicken and pat dry. Place each chicken piece between clear plastic wrap. Pound lightly with meat mallet to ⅛-inch thickness. Remove plastic wrap.

In small shallow bowl combine flour, salt and pepper. In another small shallow bowl combine bread crumbs, Parmesan cheese and paprika. In another small bowl place egg.

Cut Cheddar cheese into four 3x1x½-inch pieces. Place a cheese stick on each chicken piece. Sprinkle chicken with dried tomatoes and fines herbes. Fold in sides of chicken and tightly roll up jellyroll style. Roll in flour mixture, egg and then bread crumb mixture.

Arrange chicken rolls in ungreased shallow baking dish, seam side down. Drizzle chicken with melted margarine.

Bake in preheated 350°F **convection oven** on rack #2 or #3 offset for 16 to 18 minutes (or bake in preheated 350°F **radiant bake oven** 20 to 25 minutes) or until chicken no longer is pink and cheese begins to melt. Makes 4 servings.

To make ahead: Assemble and coat chicken rolls as directed. Cover and chill up to 4 hours. To serve, drizzle with melted margarine and bake as directed.

Nutrition facts per serving: 372 calories (46% from fat), 38 g protein, 11 g carbohydrates, 19 g fat, 1 g dietary fiber, 158 mg cholesterol, 546 mg sodium

POTATO-TOPPED CHICKEN

Shredded hash brown potatoes, seasoned with Parmesan cheese and fresh basil, bake on top of delicate chicken breasts.

Nonstick spray coating
4 skinless, boneless chicken breast halves (about 1 pound)

Topping
1 cup loose-pack frozen shredded hash brown potatoes, thawed
⅓ cup finely chopped onion
1 egg white, slightly beaten
1 tablespoon snipped fresh basil (or ½ teaspoon dried basil leaves)
2 teaspoons vegetable oil
⅛ teaspoon pepper
2 tablespoons grated Parmesan or Romano cheese
⅛ teaspoon paprika

Apple wedges (optional)
Celery leaves (optional)

Spray baking sheet with nonstick coating. Set baking sheet aside.

Rinse chicken and pat dry. Sprinkle lightly with salt and pepper. Set aside.

For topping: In medium bowl toss together hash brown potatoes and onion. Stir in egg white, basil, vegetable oil and pepper.

Place chicken pieces on baking sheet. With hands, mound some of the potato mixture on top of each chicken piece. In small bowl combine Parmesan cheese and paprika. Sprinkle over potato mixture.

Bake in preheated 425°F **convection oven** on rack #2 or #3 offset for 11 to 13 minutes (or bake in preheated 450°F **radiant bake oven** 14 to 16 minutes) or until chicken no longer is pink.

Transfer potato-topped chicken to serving platter. Garnish with apple wedges and celery leaves, if desired. Makes 4 servings.

Nutrition facts per serving: 270 calories (38% from fat), 30 g protein, 11 g carbohydrates, 11 g fat, 1 g dietary fiber, 75 mg cholesterol, 148 mg sodium

Apples

MENU

Weeknight Family Supper
Serves 4

Crispy Baked Halibut
(page 12)

Roasted New Potatoes
(page 23)

Tossed spinach and tomato salad with bottled creamy cucumber salad dressing

Rye rolls

Browned Butter Cookies
(page 31)

Take advantage of these easy-to-fix recipes to simplify workday meals. Make the cookies ahead and store them in a tightly covered container. At mealtime, just assemble the salad while the fish and potatoes bake.

CRISPY OVEN-FRIED CHICKEN

Oven-fried chicken prepared in a convection oven is so easy and tasty that you'll want to serve it often. During summer, chill the cooked chicken to take along on picnics. (Be sure to keep it thoroughly chilled until serving time.)

1 egg, beaten
3 tablespoons milk
1 cup fine saltine cracker crumbs
1 teaspoon dried thyme or marjoram leaves
½ teaspoon paprika
⅛ teaspoon pepper
2½ to 3 pounds meaty chicken pieces (breast halves, thighs and drumsticks)
3 tablespoons margarine or butter, melted
Fresh thyme or marjoram sprigs (optional)
Tomato slices, halved (optional)

In small bowl combine beaten egg and milk. In shallow dish combine cracker crumbs, dried thyme, paprika and pepper. Set aside.

Remove skin from chicken. Rinse chicken and pat dry. Dip chicken pieces, one at a time, in egg mixture, then roll in cracker mixture.

Arrange chicken pieces in greased 15x10-inch or 13x9-inch baking pan so pieces don't touch. Drizzle chicken with melted margarine.

Bake in preheated 375°F **convection oven** on rack #2 or #3 offset for 30 to 35 minutes (or bake in preheated 375°F **radiant bake oven** 45 to 55 minutes) or until chicken pieces no longer are pink and coating is golden brown.

Transfer chicken pieces to serving platter. Garnish platter with fresh thyme sprigs and tomato slices, if desired. Makes 6 servings.

Nutrition facts per serving: 358 calories (58% from fat), 32 g protein, 5 g carbohydrates, 22 g fat, 0 g dietary fiber, 133 mg cholesterol, 231 mg sodium

SPINACH-STUFFED TURKEY BREAST

Because the spinach, Swiss cheese and ham mixture is tucked between the turkey breast and the skin, each slice has an ample share of the fabulous stuffing.

Stuffing
8 ounces fresh mushrooms, coarsely chopped
½ cup chopped onion
¼ cup margarine or butter
2 packages (10 ounces each) frozen chopped spinach, thawed and well drained
¾ cup shredded Swiss cheese
½ cup diced fully cooked ham
⅛ teaspoon pepper
Dash ground nutmeg

1 5- to 5½-pound whole turkey breast
2 tablespoons margarine or butter, melted
2 tablespoons lemon juice
½ teaspoon salt
⅛ teaspoon pepper

For stuffing: In large skillet sauté mushrooms and onion in ¼ cup margarine until tender. Remove from heat; cool slightly. Stir in spinach, Swiss cheese, ham, ⅛ teaspoon pepper and the nutmeg. Set aside.

Rinse turkey breast and pat dry. Loosen skin from turkey breast, lifting carefully and pulling it back. (Use a knife if necessary.) Leave skin attached at neck end of breast. (Do not cut or tear skin.)

Spoon stuffing onto breast meat. Replace skin over stuffing. Secure skin with small skewers or wooden toothpicks. Place turkey breast upright on rack in shallow roasting pan.

In small bowl combine melted margarine, lemon juice, salt and ⅛ teaspoon pepper. Brush onto turkey breast. Insert meat thermometer into thickest portion of breast.

Bake in 325°F **convection oven** on rack #2 offset for 1¾ to 2 hours (or bake in 325°F **radiant bake oven** 2 to 2¼ hours) or until thermometer registers 170°F, brushing with pan drippings occasionally. If necessary, cover turkey breast with foil the last 30 minutes to prevent overbrowning. Let stand, covered, 10 minutes before carving. Makes 12 servings.

Nutrition facts per serving: 263 calories (31% from fat), 40 g protein, 5 g carbohydrates, 9 g fat, 2 g dietary fiber, 107 mg cholesterol, 333 mg sodium

CORN TORTILLA CASSEROLE

This cheese-packed meatless main dish boasts a double dose of corn—corn tortillas and whole-kernel corn. Serve the casserole with your favorite salsa or picante sauce.

8   corn tortillas
1½   cups shredded Monterey Jack or
        Cheddar cheese
1   cup frozen whole-kernel corn
½   cup sliced green onions
2   eggs, beaten
1   cup buttermilk
1   can (4 ounces) diced green chili
        peppers, drained
     Tomato wedges (optional)
     Fresh cilantro sprigs (optional)

Tear corn tortillas into bite-size pieces. Arrange half of the tortillas in greased 2-quart square baking dish.

Top with half of the Monterey Jack cheese, half of the frozen corn and half of the green onions. Repeat layering with remaining tortillas, cheese, corn and green onions.

In medium mixing bowl stir together beaten eggs, buttermilk and chili peppers. Gently pour egg mixture over tortilla mixture.

Bake in 325°F **convection oven** on rack #2 or #3 offset for 23 to 25 minutes (or bake in preheated 325°F **radiant bake oven** 28 to 30 minutes) or until center is set.

Let stand 10 minutes. Garnish casserole with tomato wedges and cilantro sprigs, if desired. Serve warm. Makes 4 servings.

Nutrition facts per serving: 398 calories (38% from fat), 21 g protein, 43 g carbohydrates, 18 g fat, 5 g dietary fiber, 147 mg cholesterol, 756 mg sodium

ROAST GOOSE WITH CHERRY SAUCE

The sweet-tart flavor of this spicy fruit sauce blends deliciously with poultry. Besides goose, the sauce goes wonderfully with chicken, turkey or pheasant.

1   8- to 10-pound domestic goose
2   tablespoons lemon juice

Sauce
¾   cup apple-cherry juice
⅓   cup sugar
9   inches stick cinnamon
6   whole cloves
1   tablespoon cornstarch
1   tablespoon cold water
1   package (16 ounces) frozen
        unsweetened pitted tart red cherries,
        thawed and drained
2   tablespoons brandy or kirsch

Rinse goose and pat dry. Season cavity with salt. Skewer neck skin to back. Tuck drumsticks under band of skin across tail or tie drumsticks to tail. Twist wing tips under back. Prick skin well all over.

Place goose on rack in shallow roasting pan, breast side up. Brush with lemon juice. Insert meat thermometer into center of a thigh.

Bake in 350°F **convection oven** on rack #2 offset for 1¾ to 2½ hours (or bake in 350°F **radiant bake oven** 2¾ to 3¼ hours) or until thermometer registers 180° to 185°F and drumsticks move easily. Remove fat during roasting. Let goose stand, covered, 15 minutes before carving.

Spices

For sauce: In medium saucepan combine apple-cherry juice, sugar, cinnamon and cloves. Heat to boiling; reduce heat. Cover and simmer 15 minutes. Remove spices.

Combine cornstarch and water; add to juice mixture. Cook and stir over medium heat until sauce is thickened and bubbly. Cook and stir 2 minutes more. Stir in tart red cherries and brandy; heat through.

Serve warm cherry sauce with sliced goose. Makes 10 servings.

Nutrition facts per serving: 437 calories (56% from fat), 31 g protein, 15 g carbohydrates, 27 g fat, 1 g dietary fiber, 111 mg cholesterol, 86 mg sodium

Herb-Roasted Vegetables

SIDE DISHES

From Vegetable-Topped Potato Skins to Apple Butter-Filled Muffins, these simple, satisfying side dishes from your convection oven will add new life to any meal.

HERB-ROASTED VEGETABLES

Using packaged fresh baby carrots saves work and time—they're already peeled and trimmed.

10	tiny new potatoes, halved or quartered
1½	cups peeled and trimmed baby carrots
1	small onion, cut into wedges

Seasoning
¼	cup olive oil
3	tablespoons lemon juice
3	cloves garlic, minced
1	tablespoon snipped fresh rosemary or oregano (or 1 teaspoon dried rosemary or oregano leaves)
½	teaspoon salt
¼	teaspoon pepper

½	small eggplant, quartered lengthwise and cut into ½-inch slices (2 cups)
1	medium red or green sweet pepper, cut into ½-inch-wide strips
	Fresh rosemary or oregano sprigs (optional)

Combine new potatoes, baby carrots and onion in ungreased 13x9-inch baking pan.

For seasoning: In small mixing bowl combine olive oil, lemon juice, garlic, snipped rosemary, salt and pepper. Drizzle seasoning over vegetables. Toss gently to coat.

Bake in 425°F **convection oven** on rack #2 or #3 offset for 20 minutes (or bake in preheated 450°F **radiant bake oven** 30 minutes), stirring vegetables once.

Remove from oven. Add eggplant and red sweet pepper. Toss to combine. Return to oven.

Bake 13 to 15 minutes more or until vegetables are tender and brown on edges, stirring once.

Garnish vegetables with rosemary sprigs, if desired. Makes 6 to 8 servings.

Nutrition facts per serving: 227 calories (36% from fat), 3 g protein, 34 g carbohydrates, 9 g fat, 5 g dietary fiber, 0 mg cholesterol, 214 mg sodium

ZUCCHINI AU GRATIN

Feta cheese lends a wonderfully sharp, salty flavor to this fresh-tasting squash casserole.

2	medium zucchini and/or yellow summer squash, sliced (2½ cups)
1	tablespoon margarine or butter
2	teaspoons all-purpose flour
⅛	teaspoon pepper
½	cup milk
½	cup shredded Gruyère cheese
¼	cup crumbled feta cheese
¼	cup thinly sliced green onions

Topping
¼	cup fine dry bread crumbs (unseasoned)
1	tablespoon snipped fresh parsley
1	tablespoon margarine or butter, melted
	Fresh parsley sprigs (optional)

In medium saucepan cook zucchini, covered, in small amount of boiling salted water 3 to 5 minutes or until crisp-tender. Drain well.

In another medium saucepan melt 1 tablespoon margarine. Stir in flour and pepper. Blend in milk. Cook and stir over medium heat until mixture is thickened and bubbly. Cook and stir 1 minute more.

Add the Gruyère and feta cheeses, stirring until almost melted. Stir in cooked zucchini and green onions. Transfer to ungreased 1-quart casserole.

For topping: In small bowl combine bread crumbs, snipped parsley and 1 tablespoon melted margarine. Sprinkle over zucchini mixture.

Bake in 350°F **convection oven** on rack #2 or #3 offset for 15 to 20 minutes (or bake in preheated 350°F **radiant bake oven** 20 to 25 minutes) or until topping is lightly browned. Garnish casserole with parsley sprigs, if desired. Makes 4 servings.

Nutrition facts per serving: 186 calories (61% from fat), 8 g protein, 10 g carbohydrates, 13 g fat, 1 g dietary fiber, 24 mg cholesterol, 248 mg sodium

SIDE DISHES

VEGETABLE-TOPPED POTATO SKINS

As side dish or appetizer, these crisp potato wedges filled with cheese and bacon are hard to resist.

6	medium baking potatoes (about 2 pounds)
¼	cup margarine or butter, melted

Topping

⅔	cup finely chopped red or green sweet pepper
½	cup chopped onion
¼	cup coarsely chopped pecans
2	cloves garlic, minced
1	tablespoon olive or vegetable oil
1	cup shredded process Gruyère or Cheddar cheese
4	slices bacon, cooked crisp and crumbled
2	tablespoons snipped fresh chives

Prick potato skins with tines of fork. Bake in 425°F **convection oven** on rack #2 or #3 offset for 25 to 35 minutes (or bake in 425°F **radiant bake oven** 50 to 60 minutes) or until tender.

Cut potatoes lengthwise into quarters. Scoop out insides (reserve for another use), leaving ¼-inch-thick shells. Brush both sides of potato skins with melted margarine.

Place on ungreased large baking sheet, cut side up. Bake in the 425°F **convection oven** 7 to 10 minutes (or bake in the 425°F **radiant bake oven** 10 to 15 minutes) or until crisp.

Meanwhile, for topping: In medium saucepan sauté red sweet pepper, onion, pecans and garlic in olive oil until onion is tender. Remove from heat and cool slightly.

Stir Gruyère cheese, crumbled bacon and chives into onion mixture. Spoon topping onto hot potato skins.

Return to oven and bake 1 to 2 minutes more or until cheese melts. Makes 6 servings.

Nutrition facts per serving: 410 calories (49% from fat), 12 g protein, 41 g carbohydrates, 23 g fat, 4 g dietary fiber, 28 mg cholesterol, 219 mg sodium

New Potatoes

TWICE-BAKED ACORN SQUASH

Team this hearty squash and spinach combo with chicken, turkey or pork.

2	medium acorn squash

Filling

1	package (10 ounces) frozen chopped spinach, thawed and well drained
⅓	cup grated Parmesan or Romano cheese
3	slices bacon, cooked crisp and crumbled
3	tablespoons margarine or butter, softened
2	tablespoons thinly sliced green onion
⅛	teaspoon salt
⅛	teaspoon ground red pepper

Topping

2	tablespoons soft bread crumbs
1	tablespoon grated Parmesan or Romano cheese

Halve squash lengthwise. Remove seeds. Place squash in large baking dish, cut side down.

Bake in 350°F **convection oven** on rack #2 or #3 offset for 35 to 40 minutes (or bake in preheated 350°F **radiant bake oven** 50 to 55 minutes) or until tender.

Scoop out the squash pulp, leaving ¼-inch-thick shells.

For filling: In large mixing bowl combine squash pulp, spinach, ⅓ cup Parmesan cheese, crumbled bacon, margarine, green onion, salt and red pepper. Spoon into squash shells.

For topping: In small bowl combine bread crumbs and 1 tablespoon Parmesan cheese. Sprinkle over filling.

Return squash halves, stuffed sides up, to same baking dish. Bake in the 350°F **convection oven** 20 to 25 minutes (or bake in the 350°F **radiant bake oven** 25 to 30 minutes) or until filling is heated through. Makes 4 servings.

Nutrition facts per serving: 226 calories (54% from fat), 9 g protein, 19 g carbohydrates, 14 g fat, 6 g dietary fiber, 12 mg cholesterol, 465 mg sodium

ROASTED NEW POTATOES

Serve versatile oven-roasted potatoes with your favorite grilled steaks, chops or burgers.

12	tiny new potatoes, halved, or 4 medium potatoes, cut into eighths
2	tablespoons vegetable oil
	Dash salt
2	large shallots or 4 green onions, finely chopped

Combine potatoes and vegetable oil in ungreased 2-quart rectangular baking dish. Toss gently to coat. Sprinkle with salt. Bake in 450°F **convection oven** on rack #2 or #3 offset for 10 minutes (or bake in preheated 450°F **radiant bake oven** 15 minutes).

Sprinkle with shallots. Bake 9 to 11 minutes more or until potatoes are tender and brown on edges. Makes 4 servings.

Nutrition facts per serving: 267 calories (23% from fat), 4 g protein, 48 g carbohydrates, 7 g fat, 4 g dietary fiber, 0 mg cholesterol, 48 mg sodium

CHEDDAR BATTER BREAD

Crunchy and flavorful, this easy batter bread makes wonderful toast!

1	tablespoon cornmeal
2	cups all-purpose flour
1	package (¼ ounce) quick-rising active dry yeast
1	cup milk
2	tablespoons sugar
2	tablespoons margarine or butter
¼	teaspoon onion powder
¼	teaspoon salt
¼	teaspoon pepper
1	egg
¾	cup shredded Cheddar or Monterey Jack cheese with jalapeño peppers
½	cup cornmeal

Grease 8x4-inch loaf pan. Sprinkle with 1 tablespoon cornmeal. Set aside.

In large mixing bowl combine 1½ cups flour and the yeast. In small saucepan heat and stir milk, sugar, margarine, onion powder, salt and pepper just until warm (120° to 130°F). Add mixture and egg to dry ingredients.

Beat on low speed of electric mixer until moistened. Beat 3 minutes on high speed. Stir Cheddar cheese and ½ cup cornmeal into beaten mixture. Stir in the remaining flour. (The batter will be soft and sticky.)

Pour batter into prepared loaf pan. Cover and let rise in warm place 20 minutes or until light and nearly doubled in size.

Bake in preheated 325°F **convection oven** on rack #2 or #3 offset for 30 to 35 minutes (or bake in preheated 350°F **radiant bake oven** 35 to 40 minutes) or until golden brown and loaf sounds hollow when lightly tapped.

Remove bread from pan. Cool on wire rack. Makes 1 loaf (16 servings).

Nutrition facts per serving: 128 calories (29% from fat), 4 g protein, 18 g carbohydrates, 4 g fat, 1 g dietary fiber, 20 mg cholesterol, 90 mg sodium

Cheddar Batter Bread

SIDE DISHES

POPOVERS

Serve these crispy, hollow puffs with butter or honey as a side dish. For a main dish, break the puffs in half and spoon creamed chicken or lobster Newburg over them.

1	tablespoon vegetable shortening or nonstick spray coating
2	eggs
1	cup milk
1	tablespoon vegetable oil
1	cup all-purpose flour
¼	teaspoon salt

Using ½ teaspoon shortening for each cup, grease bottom and sides of six 6-ounce custard cups or the cups of a popover pan. Or spray cups with nonstick coating. Place custard cups in 15x10-inch baking pan. Set aside.

Using wire whisk or rotary beater, in medium mixing bowl beat eggs, milk and oil until combined. Add flour and salt. Beat until smooth.

Fill prepared cups half full with batter. Bake in preheated 400°F **convection oven** on rack #2 or #3 offset for 28 to 30 minutes (or bake in preheated 400°F **radiant bake oven** 38 to 40 minutes) or until golden brown and very firm.

Immediately after removing popovers from oven, use tines of fork to prick each popover to let steam escape. Turn off oven. For crisper popovers, return popovers to the heated **convection oven** 4 to 6 minutes (or return popovers to the heated **radiant bake oven** 5 to 10 minutes) or until desired crispness is reached. Remove popovers from cups and serve immediately. Makes 6 popovers.

Nutrition facts per popover: 160 calories (40% from fat), 6 g protein, 18 g carbohydrates, 7 g fat, 1 g dietary fiber, 74 mg cholesterol, 130 mg sodium

LEMON-POPPY SEED POPOVERS: Follow the recipe above, except add 1 tablespoon *poppy seed* and 1½ teaspoons grated *lemon* or *orange peel* with the flour and salt.

Nutrition facts per popover: 168 calories (42% from fat), 6 g protein, 19 g carbohydrates, 8 g fat, 1 g dietary fiber, 74 mg cholesterol, 131 mg sodium

POTATO BREAD

Cooked potato makes this wholesome bread deliciously moist.

1½	cups water
1	medium potato, peeled and cubed
1	cup buttermilk or sour milk
3	tablespoons sugar
2	tablespoons margarine or butter
1½	teaspoons salt
6	to 6½ cups all-purpose flour
2	packages (¼ ounce each) active dry yeast

In saucepan combine water and potato. Heat to boiling. Cover and cook 12 to 14 minutes or until very tender. *Do not drain.* Mash potato in the water. Measure potato mixture. If necessary, add additional water to make 1¾ cups total. Return mixture to saucepan. Add buttermilk, sugar, margarine and salt. Heat or cool as necessary to 120° to 130°F.

In large mixing bowl combine 2 cups flour and the yeast. Add potato mixture. Beat on low speed of electric mixer until moistened. Beat 3 minutes on high speed. Stir in enough remaining flour to form moderately stiff dough.

On floured surface knead dough until smooth and elastic, 6 to 8 minutes. Shape into a ball. Place in greased bowl. Turn greased side up. Cover and let rise in warm place 45 to 60 minutes or until light and doubled in size.

Punch down dough. Turn out onto floured surface. Divide in half. Cover and let rest 10 minutes. Shape into 2 loaves. Lightly dip tops in additional flour. Place in 2 lightly greased 8x4-inch loaf pans, flour side up. Cover and let rise 30 minutes or until nearly doubled in size.

Bake in preheated 350°F **convection oven** on rack #2 or #3 offset for 25 to 30 minutes (or bake in preheated 375°F **radiant bake oven** 35 to 40 minutes) or until golden brown and loaves sound hollow when lightly tapped.

Remove from pans and cool on wire rack. Makes 2 loaves (24 servings).

Nutrition facts per serving: 139 calories (9% from fat), 4 g protein, 27 g carbohydrates, 1 g fat, 1 g dietary fiber, 0 mg cholesterol, 153 mg sodium

WHOLE-WHEAT POTATO BREAD: Follow the recipe above, except reduce all-purpose flour to 4 to 4½ cups and add 2 cups *whole-wheat flour*. Stir in whole-wheat flour along with enough remaining all-purpose flour to form moderately stiff dough.

Nutrition facts per serving: 135 calories (10% from fat), 4 g protein, 27 g carbohydrates, 1 g fat, 2 g dietary fiber, 0 mg cholesterol, 153 mg sodium

POTATO BUNS: Follow either recipe above, except divide each half of dough into 12 pieces. Shape into balls. Lightly dip tops in additional all-purpose flour. Place on 2 greased baking sheets. Cover and let rise 30 minutes or until nearly doubled in size. Bake in preheated 350°F **convection oven** on racks #2 offset and #3 for 15 to 18 minutes (or bake in preheated 375°F **radiant bake oven** 20 to 25 minutes) or until golden brown. Makes 24 buns.

Nutrition facts per bun: Same as each serving of Potato Bread or Whole-Wheat Potato Bread.

CHERRY TEA RING

Show off this daisy-shaped bread, brimming with a spicy dried-cherry filling, at your next brunch.

3⅓ to 3⅔ cups all-purpose flour
1 package (¼ ounce) active dry yeast
1 cup milk
¼ cup sugar
¼ cup margarine or butter
¾ teaspoon salt
1 egg

Filling
¼ cup sugar
¼ cup packed brown sugar
2 tablespoons all-purpose flour
1 teaspoon ground cinnamon
3 tablespoons margarine or butter
1 cup snipped dried cherries

1 recipe Vanilla Glaze (above, right)

In large mixing bowl combine 1½ cups flour and the yeast. In small saucepan heat and stir milk, ¼ cup sugar, ¼ cup margarine and the salt just until warm (120° to 130°F). Add mixture and eggs to dry ingredients.

Beat on low speed of electric mixer until moistened. Beat 3 minutes on high speed. Stir in enough of the remaining flour to form moderately stiff dough. On floured surface knead dough until smooth and elastic, 6 to 8 minutes. Shape dough into a ball. Place in greased bowl. Turn greased side up. Cover and let rise in warm place 1¼ hours or until light and doubled in size.

Meanwhile, for filling: In medium mixing bowl combine ¼ cup sugar, the brown sugar, 2 tablespoons flour and the cinnamon. With pastry blender or fork, cut in 3 tablespoons margarine until crumbly. Set aside. In bowl cover dried cherries with boiling water. Let stand 5 minutes. Drain cherries, squeezing to remove excess water.

Punch down dough. Turn out onto floured surface. Cover and let rest 10 minutes. Roll dough to form 15x9-inch rectangle. Sprinkle dough with brown sugar mixture. Sprinkle with cherries. Roll up jellyroll style, starting from a long side. Seal seams.

Place on greased large baking sheet. Attach ends to form a circle; pinch seam to seal. Using kitchen scissors or sharp knife, cut a vertical slit from outside of dough to center, leaving about 1 inch still attached at center. Repeat at 1-inch intervals around ring. Gently turn slices cut side down. Cover and let rise 30 minutes or until nearly doubled in size.

Bake in preheated 325°F **convection oven** on rack #2 or #3 offset for 25 to 30 minutes (or bake in preheated 350°F **radiant bake oven** 25 to 30 minutes) or until golden brown and top sounds hollow when lightly tapped. If necessary, cover loosely with foil the last 5 to 10 minutes to prevent overbrowning. Transfer to wire rack; cool. Drizzle with Vanilla Glaze. Makes 1 tea ring (12 servings).

VANILLA GLAZE: In small bowl stir together 1¼ cups sifted *confectioners' sugar*, 1 teaspoon *light corn syrup*, ¼ teaspoon *vanilla*, ⅛ teaspoon *almond extract* and enough *half-and-half* (1 to 2 tablespoons) until glaze reaches drizzling consistency.

Nutrition facts per serving: 333 calories (22% from fat), 6 g protein, 60 g carbohydrates, 8 g fat, 1 g dietary fiber, 20 mg cholesterol, 208 mg sodium

APPLE BUTTER-FILLED MUFFINS

Topped with sugar and crunchy pecans and filled with pleasantly sweet apple butter, these tender muffins make a sensational breakfast treat.

1¾ cups all-purpose flour
⅓ cup sugar
2 teaspoons baking powder
1 teaspoon apple pie spice or pumpkin pie spice
¼ teaspoon salt
1 egg, beaten
¾ cup milk
¼ cup vegetable oil
⅓ cup apple butter
⅓ cup chopped pecans
2 tablespoons sugar

In medium mixing bowl combine flour, ⅓ cup sugar, baking powder, apple pie spice and salt.

Combine the beaten egg, milk and vegetable oil. Add to dry ingredients. Stir just until moistened.

Lightly grease bottoms of 12 muffin cups or line with paper bake cups. Spoon a heaping tablespoon of batter into each muffin cup. Top each with a heaping teaspoon of apple butter, then with the remaining batter.

In small bowl combine chopped pecans and 2 tablespoons sugar. Sprinkle over batter.

Bake in preheated 375°F **convection oven** on rack #2 or #3 offset for 14 to 16 minutes (or bake in preheated 400°F **radiant bake oven** 18 to 20 minutes) or until golden brown. Loosen edges from pan; remove muffins. Serve warm. Makes 12 muffins.

Nutrition facts per muffin: 187 calories (37% from fat), 3 g protein, 27 g carbohydrates, 8 g fat, 1 g dietary fiber, 19 mg cholesterol, 111 mg sodium

TIPS

Yeast Bread Baking Hints

These pointers will help you turn out picture-perfect yeast loaves and rolls every time.

•*To ensure your bread rises properly, keep the yeast at just the right temperature. Use a thermometer to check the temperature of the liquid mixture. And choose a draft-free area that's between 80° and 85°F for raising your dough.*
•*When adding flour to form the dough, start by using the minimum amount specified. If the dough seems sticky during kneading, add more flour a little at a time, being careful not to go over the maximum amount.*
•*To check the dough to see if it has doubled in size, press two fingers ½ inch into the dough. If the indentations remain after you remove your fingers, the dough is ready to shape.*

Nuts

DESSERTS

Easy-to-make cookies, delicious pies, fruit-filled dumplings, a spectacular torte—with choices like these, you're sure to find just the convection-baked dessert to satisfy your sweet tooth.

CHERRY-BLUEBERRY COBBLER SUPREME

By choosing from fresh or frozen fruits, you can serve this comforting dessert both summer and winter or anytime in between.

- 2   cups fresh or frozen pitted tart red cherries
- 1   cup fresh or frozen blueberries
- 1   cup all-purpose flour
- 1   cup whole-wheat flour
- 2   teaspoons baking powder
- ¼   teaspoon salt
- 1   cup sugar
- ½   cup margarine or butter, softened
- ¾   cup milk
-     Cherry or apple juice (about 2 cups)
- ½   to ¾ cup sugar
-     Confectioners' sugar (optional)
-     Ice cream or half-and-half (optional)

Thaw fruit, if frozen. In medium mixing bowl stir together flours, baking powder and salt. In another medium mixing bowl beat 1 cup sugar and margarine until well combined. Add dry ingredients alternately with milk. Beat until smooth. Spread the batter in greased 13x9-inch baking pan.

Drain fruit, reserving liquid (only if using thawed frozen fruit). Add enough cherry juice to fruit liquid to equal 2 cups. Sprinkle cherries and blueberries over batter. Sprinkle with remaining ½ to ¾ cup sugar, depending on the sweetness of fruit. Pour the 2 cups of cherry juice mixture over the fruit.

Bake in 325°F **convection oven** on rack #2 or #3 offset for 38 to 40 minutes (or bake in preheated 350°F **radiant bake oven** 40 to 45 minutes) or until wooden toothpick inserted in cake comes out clean. (Some of the fruit should sink toward bottom as cake rises to top.)

Cool cobbler for 30 minutes. Sprinkle lightly with confectioners' sugar, if desired. Serve warm with ice cream, if desired. Makes 12 servings.

Nutrition facts per serving: 282 calories (26% from fat), 3 g protein, 50 g carbohydrates, 8 g fat, 2 g dietary fiber, 1 mg cholesterol, 172 mg sodium

BRANDIED APRICOT-PEAR DUMPLINGS

Tangy apricots and rich cream cheese blend with mild pears to make this flaky dessert.

- 2   tablespoons snipped dried apricots
- 2   tablespoons soft-style cream cheese
- 4   small pears
- 1   recipe Single-Crust Pastry, page 28
- 1   egg white, beaten with 1 tablespoon water
- 1   tablespoon sugar
- 1¼ cups pear or apricot nectar
- ¼   cup dark corn syrup
- ¼   cup brandy or pear or apricot nectar
-     Strawberry fans (optional)

In small bowl combine apricots and cream cheese. Peel and core pears, reserving stems. Spoon apricot mixture into centers of pears.

Prepare Single-Crust Pastry. On floured surface roll pastry to about a 13-inch square. Trim to an even 12-inch square. Using fluted pastry wheel or knife, cut pastry into sixteen 12x¾-inch strips.

Pat pears with paper towels. Using a pastry strip and starting ½ inch above base of pear (do not cover bottom), wrap strip around pear. Moisten end of strip and seal to end of a second strip. Continue wrapping strip around pear. Add a third strip. Finish wrapping pear, covering top. Moisten end to seal. Repeat, using 3 pastry strips on each pear. Using knife, cut leaf shapes from remaining pastry strips. Score veins on leaves. Moisten and attach leaves to tops of pears.

Brush pastry with egg white mixture. Sprinkle with sugar. Transfer to ungreased shallow baking dish. In mixing bowl stir together pear nectar, corn syrup and brandy. Pour around pears in dish. Bake in preheated 375°F **convection oven** on rack #2 or #3 offset for 40 to 45 minutes (or bake in preheated 400°F **radiant bake oven** 45 to 50 minutes) or until golden brown.

Replace stems in tops of pears. Garnish pears with strawberry fans, if desired. Serve warm. Makes 4 servings.

Nutrition facts per serving: 563 calories (32% from fat), 6 g protein, 85 g carbohydrates, 20 g fat, 6 g dietary fiber, 8 mg cholesterol, 207 mg sodium

Brandied Apricot-Pear Dumplings

MENU

*Dessert Party
Extravaganza*

Serves 8

*Sour Cream, Raisin and
Pear Pie
(opposite)*

*Almond Meringues
(page 33)*

*Fudgy Nutty Brownies
(page 30)*

Strawberries or other fresh fruits

Cappuccino or espresso

Assorted hot teas

*Set the table with your prettiest
linens, crystal and silver for this
banquet of sweets. Add a lovely
touch by placing fresh flowers in
containers of various shapes and
sizes and using them as a
centerpiece and elsewhere
throughout the room.*

*For the most part, you can
make these delicious desserts in
advance. But if pressed for time,
make just one or two of the
recipes and fill in with a
purchased dessert, assorted
candies or nuts.*

APPLES IN PHYLLO

*Jonathan, Winesap, Granny Smith and Cortland apples
have a tart flavor and firm texture that are ideal for this
glamorous adaptation of the baked apple.*

4	sheets frozen phyllo dough (18x14-inch rectangles), thawed
¼	cup margarine or butter, melted
6	small tart cooking apples
¼	cup sugar
1	teaspoon ground cinnamon
⅓	cup slivered almonds
	Vanilla ice cream (optional)
1	recipe Rum-Raisin Sauce (below)

Grease six 6-ounce custard cups so each cup is
entirely covered. Set aside.

Brush one sheet of phyllo dough with some of
the melted margarine. (Remove one sheet of
phyllo at a time and keep remaining sheets
covered with a damp paper towel.) Brush a
second sheet of phyllo with margarine and layer
on top of first sheet. Repeat brushing and
layering with remaining phyllo and margarine.

Cut phyllo lengthwise into 6 strips. Cut strips
crosswise into thirds, forming 18 rectangles each
4 phyllo layers thick. Press 3 rectangles evenly
into each custard cup.

Peel and core apples. Cut each apple into thin
slices, cutting three-fourths of the way to, but
not through, the bottom. (To prevent cutting
through the bottom, place a wooden-handled
spoon or chopstick on each side of apple.)
Repeat with remaining apples.

In small bowl combine sugar and cinnamon.
Place an apple into each phyllo-lined custard
cup. Sprinkle apples with sugar-cinnamon
mixture. Fill apple cavities with almonds. Place
custard cups in 15x10-inch baking pan.

Bake in preheated 375°F **convection oven** on
rack #2 or #3 offset for 15 to 20 minutes (or
bake in preheated 375°F **radiant bake oven** 25
to 30 minutes) or until phyllo is golden brown
and apples are tender. Cool slightly.

Carefully slip out desserts onto individual
dessert plates. Place a small scoop of vanilla ice
cream on top of each apple, if desired. Spoon
warm or cool Rum-Raisin Sauce over apples.
Makes 6 servings.

RUM-RAISIN SAUCE: In small heavy saucepan
stir together ½ cup packed *brown sugar* and
1 tablespoon *cornstarch.* Stir in ⅓ cup *water* and
⅓ cup *raisins.* Cook and stir until thickened and
bubbly. Cook and stir 2 minutes more. Stir in
1 tablespoon *rum.* Serve sauce immediately or
cover surface with clear plastic wrap; cool.

*Nutrition facts per serving: 341 calories (30% from
fat), 4 g protein, 57 g carbohydrates, 12 g fat, 4 g dietary
fiber, 0 mg cholesterol, 131 mg sodium*

PEACH CLAFOUTI WITH CITRUS SAUCE

*Luscious peaches are surrounded by a rich almond custard
in this delicate French dessert.*

2	medium peaches, peeled, pitted and sliced
2	tablespoons sugar
2	cups evaporated milk
3	eggs
¼	cup all-purpose flour
3	tablespoons sugar
½	teaspoon almond extract
½	teaspoon vanilla
	Dash salt
1	recipe Citrus Sauce (below)

Combine peaches and 2 tablespoons sugar in
ungreased 8-inch round baking dish.

In blender container combine evaporated milk,
eggs, flour, 3 tablespoons sugar, the almond
extract, vanilla and salt. Cover and blend 15
seconds. Pour over fruit.

Bake in 350°F **convection oven** on rack #2 or
#3 offset for 30 to 35 minutes (or bake in
preheated 375°F **radiant bake oven** 40 to 45
minutes) or until custard appears set when a
knife is inserted in custard near center. Serve
warm with Citrus Sauce. Makes 4 servings.

CITRUS SAUCE: In small saucepan combine
⅓ cup *sugar* and 2 teaspoons *cornstarch.* Stir in
⅔ cup *water.* Cook and stir over medium heat
until sauce is thickened and bubbly. Cook and
stir 2 minutes more. Remove from heat. Stir in
2 tablespoons *orange juice* and 1 tablespoon *lemon
juice.* Makes about 1 cup.

*Nutrition facts per serving: 408 calories (29% from
fat), 15 g protein, 58 g carbohydrates, 13 g fat, 1 g dietary
fiber, 197 mg cholesterol, 213 mg sodium*

SINGLE-CRUST PASTRY

1¼	cups all-purpose flour
¼	teaspoon salt
⅓	cup vegetable shortening
3	to 4 tablespoons cold water

In medium mixing bowl combine flour and
salt. Cut in shortening until mixture is like coarse
meal. Add water, 1 tablespoon at a time, stirring
with fork until particles are moistened and stick
together. Form pastry into a ball.

PECAN SINGLE-CRUST PASTRY: Follow the
recipe above, except stir in ¼ cup finely chopped
pecans after cutting in shortening.

SOUR CREAM, RAISIN AND PEAR PIE

For a spectacular pie with attractive slices of pear, use a firm-textured variety. In the summer and fall choose red or yellow Bartlet pears. In the winter and spring select Bosc pears.

1 recipe Single-Crust Pastry, page 28

Filling
¾ cup light raisins
3 egg yolks, beaten
1½ cups dairy sour cream
3 tablespoons all-purpose flour
1 cup sugar
½ cup milk
1 teaspoon ground cinnamon
¼ teaspoon ground cloves
¼ teaspoon ground nutmeg

2 small pears
1½ cups water
⅔ cup packed brown sugar
2 tablespoons dark corn syrup
1 tablespoon lemon juice
1 tablespoon cold water
1 teaspoon cornstarch

Prepare Single-Crust Pastry. On floured surface roll pastry to form 12-inch circle. Fit pastry into 9-inch pie plate. Trim to ¼ inch beyond edge. Fold under extra pastry.

Using knife, cut leaf shapes about 1 inch long from pastry trimmings. Score veins on leaves. Brush pastry edge with water. Gently press leaves along edge, overlapping slightly. *Do not prick pastry.* Line with double thickness of foil.

Bake in preheated 450°F **convection oven** on rack #2 or #3 offset for 5 minutes (or bake in preheated 450°F **radiant bake oven** 5 minutes). Remove foil. Bake 5 to 7 minutes more or until pastry is golden brown. Remove from oven. Reduce oven temperature to 375°F.

For filling: In small mixing bowl cover light raisins with boiling water. Let stand 5 minutes. Drain well. In medium mixing bowl combine egg yolks, sour cream and flour. Stir in raisins, 1 cup sugar, the milk, cinnamon, cloves and nutmeg. Pour filling into baked pastry shell. Cover edge with foil.

Bake in 375°F **convection oven** 15 minutes (or bake in 375°F **radiant bake oven** 20 minutes). Remove foil. Continue baking 20 to 25 minutes more or until pie appears nearly set in center when gently shaken. Cool on wire rack for about 1 hour.

Meanwhile, peel and thinly slice pears. In large saucepan combine 1½ cups water, the brown sugar, corn syrup and lemon juice. Heat to boiling. Add pears. Reduce heat. Cover and simmer 4 to 5 minutes or until tender. Drain pears, reserving ⅓ cup poaching liquid. Let pears cool slightly. Combine 1 tablespoon water and the cornstarch. Stir into reserved poaching liquid.

Cook and stir until thickened and bubbly. Cook and stir 1 minute more. Remove from heat; cool slightly.

Arrange pear slices on top of pie in a circle, overlapping slightly. Brush with thickened poaching liquid. Cool completely. To store, cover and chill up to 24 hours. Makes 8 servings.

Nutrition facts per serving: 505 calories (35% from fat), 6 g protein, 79 g carbohydrates, 20 g fat, 3 g dietary fiber, 100 mg cholesterol, 115 mg sodium

CRUMB-TOPPED PEACH PIE WITH PECAN PASTRY

Peaches and pecans make a superb combination, but you also can use walnuts, hazelnuts or toasted almonds in the flaky pastry for an equally delicious pie.

1 recipe Pecan Single-Crust Pastry, page 28

Filling
½ cup sugar
3 tablespoons all-purpose flour
¼ teaspoon ground allspice or ginger (optional)
6 cups peeled and thinly sliced peaches or nectarines

Topping
½ cup all-purpose flour
½ cup packed brown sugar
3 tablespoons margarine or butter

Prepare Pecan Single-Crust Pastry. On floured surface roll pastry to form 12-inch circle. Fit pastry into 9-inch pie plate. Trim to ½ inch beyond edge. Fold under extra pastry. Flute edge. *Do not prick* pastry.

For filling: In large mixing bowl stir together sugar, 3 tablespoons flour and the allspice, if desired. Add peaches. Toss gently until coated with sugar mixture. Transfer to pie plate.

For topping: In medium mixing bowl combine ½ cup flour and the brown sugar. With pastry blender or fork, cut in margarine until crumbly. Sprinkle over filling. Cover edge with foil.

Bake in preheated 375°F **convection oven** on rack #2 or #3 offset for 25 minutes (or bake in preheated 375°F **radiant bake oven** 30 minutes). Remove foil. Bake 18 to 20 minutes more or until topping is golden brown and peaches are tender. Makes 8 servings.

Nutrition facts per serving: 385 calories (36% from fat), 4 g protein, 59 g carbohydrates, 16 g fat, 3 g dietary fiber, 0 mg cholesterol, 107 mg sodium

DESSERTS

Brown and Granulated Sugars

29

FUDGY NUTTY BROWNIES

*Indulge in the ultimate brownie. Just add a swirl of
whipped cream and a dusting of shaved chocolate and you
have pure decadence.*

Base

4	ounces unsweetened chocolate, chopped
½	cup margarine or butter
1	cup all-purpose flour
¼	teaspoon baking powder
1½	cups sugar
3	eggs
½	cup chopped walnuts or pecans, toasted
1	teaspoon vanilla

Topping

3	ounces semisweet chocolate, chopped
2	packages (3 ounces each) cream cheese
1	egg
¼	cup sugar
1	tablespoon milk
½	teaspoon vanilla
2	ounces semisweet chocolate (optional)
1	teaspoon shortening (optional)
	Fresh raspberries (optional)
	Fresh mint sprigs (optional)

For base: In small saucepan melt unsweetened
chocolate and margarine over low heat, stirring
occasionally. Remove from heat; cool.

In medium mixing bowl stir together flour and
baking powder. Set aside.

In large mixing bowl stir together melted
chocolate mixture and 1½ cups sugar. Add
3 eggs, the walnuts and 1 teaspoon vanilla. Using
wooden spoon, lightly beat mixture just until
combined. *Do not overbeat.* Stir in dry ingredients.

Spread batter in greased and lightly floured
9-inch square baking pan. Bake in preheated
325°F **convection oven** on rack #2 or #3 offset
for 22 minutes (or bake in preheated 350°F
radiant bake oven 30 minutes).

Meanwhile, for topping: In small saucepan melt
3 ounces semisweet chocolate over low heat,
stirring occasionally. Remove from heat; cool
slightly. In medium mixing bowl beat cream
cheese on medium speed of electric mixer until
softened. Add melted semisweet chocolate, 1 egg,
¼ cup sugar, the milk and ½ teaspoon vanilla.
Beat until combined.

Carefully spread topping evenly over hot
brownie base. Bake in 325°F **convection oven**
8 to 10 minutes more (or bake in 350°F **radiant
bake oven** 13 to 15 minutes more) or until
topping is set. Cool in pan on wire rack. Cover
and chill at least 2 hours.

To serve, cut into triangles or bars. In saucepan
melt 2 ounces chocolate and shortening, if
desired. Drizzle over brownies. Garnish with
raspberries and mint sprigs, if desired.

To store, cover and chill brownies. Makes
12 to 16 servings.

*Nutrition facts per serving: 409 calories (52% from
fat), 6 g protein, 46 g carbohydrates, 25 g fat, 2 g dietary
fiber, 87 mg cholesterol, 137 mg sodium*

CARROT AND ZUCCHINI BARS

Bite into these moist bar cookies and you'll discover flavors a little like carrot cake and a little like zucchini bread.

1½	cups all-purpose flour
¾	cup packed brown sugar
1	teaspoon baking powder
½	teaspoon ground ginger
¼	teaspoon baking soda
2	eggs, slightly beaten
1½	cups shredded carrot
1	cup shredded zucchini
½	cup raisins
½	cup chopped walnuts
½	cup vegetable oil
¼	cup honey
1	teaspoon vanilla
1	recipe Citrus Cream Cheese Frosting (below)
	Ground walnuts (optional)

In large mixing bowl combine flour, brown sugar, baking powder, ginger and baking soda.

In another large mixing bowl stir together eggs, carrot, zucchini, raisins, chopped walnuts, vegetable oil, honey and vanilla. Add carrot mixture to dry ingredients, stirring just until combined.

Spread batter in ungreased 13x9-inch baking pan. Bake in preheated 325°F **convection oven** on rack #2 or #3 offset for 18 to 20 minutes (or bake in preheated 350°F **radiant bake oven** 23 to 25 minutes) or until wooden toothpick inserted in center comes out clean.

Cool on wire rack. Frost with Citrus Cream Cheese Frosting. Dust with ground walnuts, if desired. To store, cover and chill. Cut into bars. Makes 36 bars.

CITRUS CREAM CHEESE FROSTING: In large mixing bowl beat together 2 packages (3 ounces each) *cream cheese*, ½ cup softened *margarine* or *butter*, 1 tablespoon grated *lemon* or *orange peel* and 2 teaspoons *vanilla* until light and fluffy. Gradually add 2 cups sifted *confectioners' sugar*, beating well.

Gradually beat in 2½ to 2¾ cups additional sifted *confectioners' sugar* until frosting reaches spreading consistency.

Nutrition facts per bar: 177 calories (43% from fat); 2 g protein, 24 g carbohydrates, 9 g fat, 1 g dietary fiber, 17 mg cholesterol, 57 mg sodium

BROWNED BUTTER COOKIES

These tender cookies, topped with creamy Browned Butter Icing, go splendidly with a glass of cold milk.

2½	cups all-purpose flour
1	teaspoon baking soda
½	teaspoon baking powder
¼	teaspoon salt
1½	cups packed brown sugar
½	cup margarine or butter
2	eggs
1	teaspoon vanilla
1	carton (8 ounces) dairy sour cream
1	cup coarsely chopped walnuts
1	recipe Browned Butter Icing (below)

In medium mixing bowl stir together flour, baking soda, baking powder and salt.

In large mixing bowl beat brown sugar and margarine on medium speed of electric mixer until well combined. Beat in eggs and vanilla until fluffy. Add dry ingredients to margarine mixture along with sour cream, mixing well. Stir in walnuts.

Drop by heaping teaspoons, 2 inches apart, onto 3 ungreased cookie sheets. Bake in preheated 325°F **convection oven** on racks #1, #3 offset and #4 for 7 to 8 minutes (or bake in preheated 350°F **radiant bake oven** 9 to 10 minutes) or until cookies are set.

Red Raspberries

Remove from cookie sheets and cool on wire racks. Frost with Browned Butter Icing. Makes about 54 cookies.

BROWNED BUTTER ICING: In medium saucepan heat ⅓ cup *butter* (not margarine) over medium-low heat 10 to 12 minutes or until lightly browned. Remove from heat.

Stir in 2½ cups sifted *confectioners' sugar* and enough *boiling water* (2 to 3 tablespoons) until icing reaches spreading consistency. Frost cookies immediately. If frosting becomes grainy, add a few drops of hot water.

Nutrition facts per cookie: 105 calories (45% from fat), 1 g protein, 14 g carbohydrates, 5 g fat, 0 g dietary fiber, 13 mg cholesterol, 60 mg sodium

PINEAPPLE UPSIDE-DOWN CAKE

The buttery caramel topping adds to the tantalizing flavor of this easy-to-make cake.

Topping

2	tablespoons margarine or butter
⅓	cup packed brown sugar
1	tablespoon water
5	or 6 pineapple slices, drained and halved
4	maraschino cherries, halved

1⅓	cups all-purpose flour
⅔	cup sugar
2	teaspoons baking powder
⅔	cup milk
¼	cup margarine or butter, softened
1	egg
1	teaspoon vanilla

For topping: Melt 2 tablespoons margarine in ungreased 9-inch round baking pan. Stir in brown sugar and water. Arrange pineapple and cherries in pan. Set aside.

In medium mixing bowl stir together flour, sugar and baking powder. Add milk, ¼ cup margarine, the egg and vanilla. Beat on low speed of electric mixer until combined. Beat on medium speed for 1 minute. Pour batter into pan over pineapple slices.

Bake in preheated 325°F **convection oven** on rack #2 or #3 offset for 30 to 35 minutes (or bake in preheated 350°F **radiant bake oven** 30 to 35 minutes) or until wooden toothpick inserted near center comes out clean.

Cool cake in pan on wire rack 5 minutes. Loosen sides and invert cake onto a plate. Serve warm. Makes 8 servings.

Nutrition facts per serving: 291 calories (30% from fat), 4 g protein, 48 g carbohydrates, 10 g fat, 1 g dietary fiber, 28 mg cholesterol, 173 mg sodium

APRICOT UPSIDE-DOWN CAKE: Follow the recipe above, except substitute 1 can (8¾ ounces) *apricot halves*, drained and halved, or *peach slices*, drained, and 2 tablespoons toasted *coconut* for pineapple and cherries.

Nutrition facts per serving: 288 calories (31% from fat), 4 g protein, 46 g carbohydrates, 10 g fat, 1 g dietary fiber, 28 mg cholesterol, 174 mg sodium

Cherries

RICE PUDDING WITH RUM-CARAMEL SAUCE

Remember this rich caramel sauce the next time you want to dress up yellow or spice cake. It's great drizzled over squares of warm cake.

4	eggs, beaten
2	cups milk or half-and-half
½	cup sugar
1	teaspoon vanilla
¼	teaspoon salt
1½	cups cooked rice, cooled
½	to ¾ cup raisins
⅛	teaspoon ground nutmeg
⅛	teaspoon ground cinnamon
1	recipe Rum-Caramel Sauce (below) Orange peel curls (optional)

Combine beaten eggs, milk, sugar, vanilla and salt in ungreased 2-quart casserole. Beat until combined but not foamy. Stir in rice and raisins.

Place casserole in 13x9-inch baking pan. Pour boiling water into the baking pan around casserole to a depth of 1 inch.

Bake in 325°F **convection oven** on rack #2 or #3 offset for 25 minutes (or bake in preheated 325°F **radiant bake oven** 25 minutes). Stir well. Sprinkle with nutmeg and cinnamon. Bake 25 to 30 minutes more or until knife inserted near center comes out clean.

Spoon warm pudding into dessert dishes. Drizzle with warm Rum-Caramel Sauce.

(Or cover and chill pudding up to 3 days. Spoon into dessert dishes and drizzle with warm Rum-Caramel Sauce.)

Garnish each serving with an orange peel curl, if desired. Makes 8 servings.

RUM-CARAMEL SAUCE: In heavy saucepan combine ½ cup packed *brown sugar* and 1 tablespoon *cornstarch*. Stir in ⅓ cup *half-and-half*, ¼ cup *water* and 2 tablespoons *dark corn syrup* or 1 tablespoon *molasses.*

Cook and stir until sauce is thickened and bubbly. (Mixture may appear curdled.) Cook and stir 2 minutes more. Remove from heat. Stir in 1 tablespoon *margarine* or *butter* and 1 tablespoon *rum* or 1 teaspoon *rum flavoring.* Makes 1 cup.

Nutrition facts per serving: 280 calories (20% from fat), 7 g protein, 49 g carbohydrates, 6 g fat, 1 g dietary fiber, 115 mg cholesterol, 158 mg sodium